How Far Is Heaven?

How Far Is Heaven?

Story by Kathleen Gorman

Paintings by Maggui Ledbetter

Barn Owl Media

Clovis, California

Mikey looked up and wondered just how far it was to heaven. He threw a kiss.

"Hey Grandma, are you ready? Here comes another one," and threw more kisses high into the air.

"Mikey, what are you doing?" his mother asked.

"I'm throwing kisses to Grandma."

"But Mikey, Grandma's in Heaven now."

"I know. She can still catch my kisses, can't she?"

"Oh Honey, I'm not sure she can."

"Why not, Mom?"

"Well... maybe she's too busy watching over
you and your cousins."

"Can I go to Heaven? I want to see Grandma."

"You can't just go to heaven. You need to be invited."

Mikey tilted his head up, staring at the clouds.

"Who invited Grandma?"

"God invited her."

"So, God wanted Grandma to visit?"

"Yes, Mikey, He did."

"Do you know what Heaven is like?"

"I really don't know, but I think Heaven is a place of no more pain. Remember how hard it was for Grandma to breathe?" Mikey nodded.

"Take a deep breath."

Mikey looked at his mother, and following her example, he took a big deep breath.

"Like this?" he asked.

"Yes, just like that. Grandma can breathe just like that now."

"So, Grandma is in a nice place now, and she can breathe without her machine? Do you think she's having fun?"

"Oh yes, I think Grandma is having lots of fun."

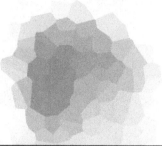

"Is Heaven far away?"

"Heaven can't be measured like a walk around
the block, or a trip to the store."

"Can I run to Heaven? Can I fly?"

"We can't run or fly either."

"So, how far is it?"

"I think Heaven might be as far as the farthest star in the sky, or as close as the memories you hold in your heart."

"Then Heaven is right here? 'Cause Grandma's in my heart?"

"That's right, Heaven just might be right here," she said smiling as she touched his heart.

This story is dedicated to the memory of my mom and dad who will always be in my heart no matter how much time has lapsed. I want to thank my family for their understanding, patience, and support. The members of my writing for pub group and our fearless leader, Janice Stevens who have willingly listened and critiqued every story I have penned. I also want to thank Dan and Peggy for believing in me and Josh for his awesome computer skills.

Most important, a special thank you to Mikey who willingly shared his name for the boy in my story.

- Kathy

I dedicate this book to my beloved grand nephew, Liam Hugh McCullough, who has taught me much in his first year of life.

Many thanks also go to Pat Hunter, artist and gallery owner, who has the heart of a great teacher. Thanks also go to George Peaden, my husband, for his help combining the images on the computer.

- Maggui

How Far Is Heaven?

Original story by Kathleen Gorman
Original artwork by Maggui Ledbetter
Book design and layout by Joshua Muster, Barn Owl Media
Barn Owl Media is a wholly owned imprint of HBE Publishing, Clovis, CA, www.hbepublishing.com

Library of Congress Control Number: 2015945086

Orders, inquiries, and correspondence should be addressed to:

HBE Publishing
info@hbepublishing.com
www.hbepublishing.com/

Printed in September 2015 in the USA

Hardback ISBN 978-1-943050-06-2
Paperback ISBN 978-1-943050-05-5

HBE PUBLISHING   Barn Owl Media

CPSIA information can be obtained at www.ICGtesting.com
Printed in the USA
LVOW05*2232290915

456281LV00015B/71/P